The Gospel of Philip

Edition by
Vladimir Antonov

Translated into English by
Anton Teplyy
and Mikhail Nikolenko

2008

ISBN 978-1438217079

This book presents a full and competent translation of the Gospel written by apostle Philip — a personal Disciple of Jesus Christ, Who attained Divinity thanks to help from Jesus. The translation is accommpanied by clarifying commentaries.

In the Gospel, Philip put the emphasis on the methodological aspect of spiritual work.

The book is addressed to everyone aspiring to Perfection.

www.swami-center.org
www.teachings-of-jesus-christ.org

Preface

The Apocryphal (i.e. not included in the New Testament) Gospel of Apostle Philip, a personal disciple of Jesus Christ, was found by archaeologists in 1945 in Egypt. It contains very important information imparted to Philip by Jesus Christ.

It concerns the highest meditative techniques bringing spiritual warriors to the Abode of God-the-Father, which Philip calls the *Bridal Chamber*. In the Gospel, two narration lines are interwoven: the line of sexual love between people and the line of the highest Love for God, the former is considered as a prototype of the latter.

The Gospel is written in artistic literary language and is rich in parables.

It was not known to Russian-speaking readers until now. Three previous editions published in thematic collections were made by translators who did not understand the meaning of the text. They made just attempts to translate the text "literally", and as a result, the translations were obscure series of words not related with each other.

The work on creating this edition was done at the request and with the help of the Author of the Gospel. The prototype of this edition of the translation is the editions [3,4]. The commentaries to the text of the Gospel are typed in small print.

The Gospel of Philip

1. A Hebrew makes a Hebrew, and such a person is called a proselyte. But a proselyte does not make a proselyte.

Those Who came from the Truth are as They were initially. And They beget other Men of Truth. The latter need only to be born (in It).

Proselyte is a person who recently accepted faith.

Those Who came from the Truth are Those Who came from the Abode of God-the-Father. They can lead Their disciples into this Abode, thus allowing them to be "born" in It.

2. A slave can hope only to become free. A slave cannot expect to inherit the estate of the master.

Yet a Son is not only a Son, but also a Co-owner of His Father's estate.

A Son of God-the-Father, coessential to Him, is a Co-owner of His property.

3. There are those who inherit the perishable. They belong to the perishable, and thus they inherit the perishable.

Those Who inherit the Imperishable are imperishable. They become owners of both the Imperishable and the perishable.

People of the perishable inherit (really) nothing. Because what can a perishable man inherit?

If the one who leaves the body inherits the True Life, it means that such One is not dead but will live.

The One Who has attained the Father through efforts on self-development achieves the True Life after the death of the body. He or She becomes a Co-owner with the Father both of the Heavenly and of the earthly.

4. A pagan does not die because has not (really) lived. So, there is no point in speaking about a pagan's death.

But those who have accepted the Truth begin to live, and there is a danger of dying for them because they live.

To die in this context means to go astray from the Path to the Father. This is a spiritual death.

5. Since the day of Christ's incarnation, the prosperity came, the cities revived, the death moved away.

6. When we were Hebrews, each of us had only a mother. But since we became Christians, we have both the Father and mother.

In the Judaic tradition, God was called *Father*. And Jesus suggested to His followers that they call only God — *Father*, not the earthly parent.

Philip says that the true followers of Christ have now the True Father.

7. Those who sow in winter reap in summer.

The winter is the earthly, but the summer is another eon. Let us sow on the Earth in winter so that we may reap the harvest in summer!

Therefore, we should not pray to God for the winter, because the winter is followed by the summer.

But the one who tries to reap in winter will not really reap but only pluck out the sprouts.

In warm regions, people sow in winter, not in spring as it is done in cold regions.

The Greek word *eons* denotes spatial dimensions; among them are those called hell, paradise, the abode of the Creator.

In "winter", i.e. while we are on the Earth, we have to work in order that in "summer" we live in sufficiency and bliss of the highest eons.

8. The one who does not follow this — will not reap the harvest. Moreover, such one will not only be without the harvest, but will have no strength in the Sabbath.

The one who does not work hard to make oneself better during the entire incarnation will not receive good fruits after it.

Philip symbolizes the period of time allocated for this work with the images of "winter" and "workweek"; then the time for rest comes — "summer", "Sabbath-Saturday" (Saturday is the Jewish day of rest).

9. Christ came to "ransom" some: to liberate, to save. He "ransomed" strangers making them His own.

Afterwards, He set apart His own — those whom He ransomed by His will.

He laid down Himself (on the Path of sacrificial service) when He Himself willed it — not only when He revealed Himself to people, but from the very day of the Creation of the World, He laid down Himself.

He was embodied, and afterwards He — when He willed — withdrew Himself. He was in the hands of robbers and was taken captive. He liberated Himself and saved also those who were regarded as good and bad in this world.

10. Light and darkness, life and death, right and left — are brothers of one another; they are inseparable (in earthly people). Because of this, among them — the good are not good, the bad are not bad, and their life is not life, and their death is not death.

So, one should begin with separating all these in oneself.

Those who have detached themselves from the earthly become whole, eternal.

The one who has entered on the spiritual Path has to separate in oneself the true, eternal, valuable for life in the highest eons — from the false, which belongs only to this world. Then one has to cultivate in oneself the first and get rid of the second.

Those Who have accomplished this become eternal in the Divine eons.

11. The importance attached to earthly things is a great delusion, for they divert our thoughts from the One Who is eternal to that which is transient. And in this case, the one who hears about God does not perceive (behind this word) the Eternal, but thinks about the transient. In the same way, behind the words *the Father, the Son, the Holy Spirit, the Life, the Light, the Resurrection,* and *the Church* — people do not perceive the Eternal, but think about the tran-

sient, unless they have already cognized the Eternal (through personal spiritual experience). These words are only misleading to earthly people.

If they were in the (Divine) eons, they would not use these words among earthly concerns and things, because these notions are related to the (Divine) eons.

In the same way, in Russia many people use the exclamation "Lord!" as a swear word in situations when other similar people use obscene language.

And God-the-Father, Who is the Universal Ocean of the Primordial Consciousness, is pictured on Orthodox icons as an old man sitting on a cloud.

Hardly one of the "pastors", not to mention the "flock", can answer the question "Who is the Holy Spirit?".

Most "believers", as well as atheists, understand the word *life* only as life in a body, mourning those who left their bodies, pitying them...

12. One name is not uttered among the earthly — the name which the Father grants to a Son. It is above all. This name is the Father. The Son would not have gotten this name if He had not become the Father.

Those who bear this name know this, but They do not speak about this. But those who do not bear this name do not know Them.

Names in this world are invented because it is not possible to cognize the Truth without them.

The Truth is one, but It is presented as Multitude. This is for our sake: to lead us to the cognition of the One through love for Multitude.

People who have not cognized the Father personally are not capable of seeing, recognizing a Son. And if a Son tries to speak to them about His coessentiality to the Father, such people only become angry with Him.

13. The earthly rulers wanted to deceive people, since they understood that people have the same origin with the really worthy. They took good names and gave these names to bad things in order to deceive people and bind them to the bad in this way. And now these earthly rulers suggest to people that they keep away from the "bad" and cling to the "good". These earthly rulers strive to make formerly free men slaves forever.

14. There are powers which give (power) to people, not wishing to save them. They do this (in order to subjugate them).

People, wishing to be saved, made sacrifices. But a reasonable one (understands clearly that) sacrifices are not necessary and animals should not be offered to deities. In fact, those who offered animals as a sacrifice were themselves like animals (by the level of their development)…

When a sacrifice was made (animals were offered to deities). Though animals were offered alive, they died.

But the one who offers oneself dead to God — (verily) will live.

Here, the last paragraph needs to be commented.

The fact is that man is not a body. Man is a consciousness, a soul. So, it is wrong to say that man is dead if the body has died. It is the body that died, but the man did not.

One can also consider death of man (as a soul, i.e. spiritual death) in the sense implied by the words of Jesus: "Follow Me, and let the dead bury their dead!" (Matt 8:22; Luke 9:60).

But in this part of His Gospel, Philip means another death — the death of one's lower individual self, and this implies the realization of the Higher Self, i.e. Mergence of the developed consciousness with the Creator. Such a person attains the Eternal Life in the Abode of the Creator in Mergence with Him.

15. Before Christ came, there was no bread of Heaven. It was like in paradise at the time of Adam: there were many trees — food for animals, but no wheat — food for man. Man used to feed like animals.

But when a Christ — Perfect Man — comes, He brings the bread from Heaven so that people may eat human food.

People without the true knowledge about their predestination and the Path, live a life quite comparable to the life of animals. God, through a Christ, gives them spiritual food appropriate to humans.

16. The earthly rulers thought that what they did they did by their own power and will. But in reality the Holy Spirit in secret accomplished all that through them — accomplished as He considered appropriate.

Also They sow everywhere the true knowledge, which existed since the beginning. And many people see it while it is being sown, but only a few of them recall about it by the time of the harvest.

The Holy Spirit directs the deeds of people when necessary. But people usually are not aware of this.

In particular, He — through vicious people — creates for other people difficulties in the form of temptations, enticements, such as false doctrines, for example. This is done for the sake of intellectual development of embodied people. After all, they are sent here to learn, not just to live.

The meaning of our lives on the Earth consists in our self-development, which must go in three main directions: intellectual, ethical, and psychoenergetical. And our Teacher is God.

Diligent students, after graduating from this School, are invited by the Father, if they deserve, to His Abode to merge there with Him forever.

But remedial students remain forever "repeaters", become slaves of this world.

The time of the "harvest" is the *end of the world:* the School is closed, the worthy students move to the Abode of the Father, enriching Him with Themselves; the lot of the rest is the *outer darkness*: destruction, death of the souls.

... A special comment has to be made concerning the use of the pronoun *They* with regard to the Holy Spirit in this fragment. This is not an error: the Holy Spirit is indeed an aggregate of former humans who attained in their development the right to be in the Highest eons.

17. Some said that Mary conceived by the Holy Spirit. They are in error. They do not understand what they say. When did a woman ever conceive by a woman?

Mary at the same time is the immaculacy, which was not defiled by violence.

She is a great temptation to Hebrews, both to those who preach and to those who listen to their preaching.

Her immaculacy, which was not defiled by violence, is pure. But the mighty of this world defiled themselves (through their fantasies).

And the Lord (Jesus Christ) would not have said, "My Father Who is in Heaven," if He had not another father. He would have said simply: "My father".

In Greek, in which the Gospel was written, the Holy Spirit is of feminine gender. This is the reason for the irony of Philip in the beginning of the fragment.

18. The Lord said to the disciples, "Enter the House of the Father. But do not take anything in the House of the Father, nor carry anything out."

The last phrase of Jesus is a joke, because in "the House of the Father" — in the highest eon — there are no material objects that can be carried out as from the house of an earthly father.

But to enter the Abode of the Heavenly Father and to settle there forever is the Goal of the evolution of every person.

19. Jesus is a human name. Christ is a title. For this reason the name Jesus is not found in other languages; He was just named Jesus.

Christ in Syriac is Messiah; Christ is a Greek word. Other languages also have this word — according to their spelling.

The Nazarene means "The One Who came from the Truth".

Christ is not the last name of Jesus as some believers think. Christ is the One Who attained the Abode of the Father, became a Part of Him, and then came to the Earth as a Divine Teacher coessential to the Father.

Christ, Messiah, Avatar — all these are just different expressions of the same phenomenon in different languages.

Jesus Christ was one, but there were many Christs throughout the entire history of mankind. Jesus was the only and the first Christ for those people with whom He communicated directly during His earthly life.

20. Christ has everything in Himself: both human and angelic, and even more mysterious, and the Father.

In the Gospel of John, there is a statement of Jesus where He compared Himself with a vine: its trunk is above the surface of the Earth, and its root comes from the Abode of the Father. Since He, as a Consciousness, is present everywhere, He can veraciously tell people about the highest eons and represent the Father in the material world.

21. They who say that the Lord died first and then rose up are in error, for He rose up first and then died (by the body).

The one who has attained the Resurrection will not die. For God lives and will be living always.

The true Resurrection is the Resurrection in the highest eons, and not in the world of matter. Jesus attained this a long time ago and came to the Earth as a Part of God-the-Father.

The One Who has traversed the Path up to Mergence with God-the-Father — attains the true immortality and after the death of the body rises in the eon of the Father in Mergence with Him.

But Jesus "rose" for embodied people in this world also, materializing every time a new body. He could do this by His Divine Power.

22. One never hides a thing of great value in a large vessel, but very often countless treasures are placed into a vessel worth an assarion. It is the same with the soul. Being a precious thing, it is placed in a contemptible body.

Atheists as well as most of those who call themselves Christians believe that man is a body.

But in reality man is a soul, a consciousness. And the body is just a temporal container, in which man has to go through the next stage of studying in the School in the material world.

Incarnate states of people are usually much shorter parts of their lives as compared to non-incarnate states.

However, the development of man can take place only in the incarnate state. It is for this reason that incarnations are necessary, it is for this reason that God creates material worlds.

The point is that the body is a "factory" for transformation of energy. In the body, the energy extracted, first of all, from ordinary food can become the energy of the consciousness, of the soul. It is thanks to this that the process of qualitative and quantitative growth of the consciousness can take place.

23. There are people who are afraid of rising naked. This is because they want to rise in the flesh. Yet they do not understand that those who wear the flesh are naked (in front of spirits and God).

But those who undress themselves (of the flesh) in order to become naked (i.e. "naked" souls) — they are not naked anymore.

Neither flesh nor blood can enter the Abode of God.

So, what is that which will not enter? It is that which is on us.

And what is that which will enter? It is that which belongs to Jesus and to His Blood.

Therefore, He said, "They who will not eat My Flesh and drink My Blood will not have the (true) life in them".

What is His Flesh? — Logos. And His Blood is the Holy Spirit. The one who has received These has true food, drink, and clothing. And I cannot agree if somebody says that This Flesh will not rise.

So, people got confused. If you say that the Flesh will not rise, then tell me, so that I may honor you as a reasonable person, what will rise?

You better say that the Spirit is this Flesh and the Light is this Flesh. And Logos is also this Flesh. So, all what you mentioned is this Flesh. And one must rise in this very Flesh, since everything is in It.

In this fragment, Philip uses a typical of the Gospel a "play on words" as a means for stimulating the reader's thinking.

Philip begins this fragment with scoffing at the fear of rising naked: the shame of nakedness of the body is not an objectively significant ethical law, but just a moral norm of certain groups of people embodied on the Earth. There are no such "norms of behavior" in the highest eons.

And in fact, God, as well as spirits, does not possess any sex (gender), because sex is peculiar to the flesh. A consciousness of any level of development is energy existing in particular eons.

Individual Consciousnesses in the Abode of the Creator abide in the mutually dissolved, merged state, forming a Whole. However, They can separate again as Individualities with the purpose of performing a specific tasks in the Creation.

Spirits retain their separateness, as well as the appearance and tendencies, habitual for them in the last incarnation. But they also can transform into a lump of energy or assume for a time someone else's appearance when they converse with embodied people.

God and spirits hear not only the words which we say but also our thoughts, even the most "secret" ones.

They also see everything existing in the world of matter, in all detail. Not only clothes, under which we hide our bodies, but even the intestines of our bodies are absolutely open to the sight of any non-incarnate being.

But embodied people usually do not know about this, do not notice, and even if they knew and noticed, they would not have a chance to hide their nakedness. We are naked before the whole Ocean of non-incarnate universal Consciousness and before many individual consciousnesses. We are visible to all. They examine us, admiring or compassionating, respecting or making fun, loving or hating, despising, foretasting our future suffering... But we do not know this, and even if we knew — anyway we do not have any place where to go, where to hide...

... Then Philip proceeds with discussing that which Jesus allegorically called His Flesh and Blood.

Jesus-"Vine", for incarnating in a body, "stretched" a part of Himself-Consciousness from the eon of the Father — to the world of matter. And He explained to the disciples that the Path to the Father consists for them in transformation of themselves into similar "Vines", but they have to grow in the direction opposite as compared to Jesus: not from the Father — to the matter, but from the matter — to the Father.

The one who grows by the "roots" to the Abode of the Father and merges there with Him in the embrace of Love — becomes a Christ with time.

In order to traverse this Path, one has to "eat" that "food" which is provided to people from the eons of the Holy Spirit and the Father. This is the "food" of the Divine knowledge. And "Logos" (i.e. "Speaking One") is the One Who brings this knowledge.

The one who gets born in the highest eons during the life in a material body and who grows one's own Divine "Flesh" in these eons is a true follower of Christ, a true Christian to become a Christ. After the death of the body, such a person truly rises, attains immortality, and for sure will not die even at the *end of the world*.

24. In this world, people mark themselves in the society by their garments.

But in the Kingdom of Heaven, the garments of the chosen are on Those Who robed themselves in the Flow and Fire, on Those Who purified Themselves.

The Flow is motion of the Consciousness of the Holy Spirit, one's entering in it is similar to submersion in a cosmic river of Living Divine Consciousness. Different variations of this meditation are called Latihan and Pranava (see more details in [1]). This represents the real baptism in the Holy Spirit. As we see, it is not similar at all to what is understood as baptism in various sects.

The Holy Spirit pervades all layers of the multidimensional Creation. A Manifestation of the Holy Spirit above the Earth's surface can be associated with a Flow. His Manifestation inside the planet is designated by Philip as Light. Another Manifestations of Him is Fire. And the Perfect Light is God-the-Father in His Abode — in the Bridal Chamber.

Baptism, performed sequentially in each of these layers, provides the next stages of purification and refinement of the consciousness of a spiritual warrior.

25. Usually obvious things are cognized through the obvious, and secret things — through the secret. But in some cases, the secret is symbolized through images of the obvious.

Thus come the image of water in the Flow and the image of fire at the blessing (of the Father).

26. Jesus conquered the hearts of people without revealing His Essence. To everyone He revealed Himself as much as they could comprehend. He did this so: to the great He appeared as great, to the small He appeared as small, to angels — as an angel, and to people — as a man. At the same time, His Divinity was hidden from all. Some, seeing Him, thought that they saw a person equal to them.

But when He revealed Himself to His disciples in the whole glory on the mountain — at that moment He was not small but truly Great. But before this, He made His disciples great, so that they could see His Greatness.

On that day, thanking the Father, He said: "O He, Who united His Perfection and Light with the Holy Spirit, unite us also with the images of angels!"

In this saying of Jesus there is a "play on words". Its meaning is: "Do so that the disciples, at last, become looking like angels!". Behind these words of Jesus there is a regret that even some of His closest disciples could not comprehend Him.

One of the peculiarities of people's development is that souls, embodied by God in human bodies, have a very different age, which does not correlate with the age of the body. This determines, first of all, the ability to comprehend information of different levels of complexity (and to a much lesser degree it depends on the age of the body, the nature of upbringing, education, and so on). Souls become mature during many incarnations, about this Jesus, as well as the apostles, told.

A wise teacher provides help to people taking into account the peculiarities of their age and their abilities to comprehend. A teacher should not give to the students information which is too complex and beyond their comprehending abilities.

The spiritual Path is like a stairway consisting of many steps. And it is necessary to help disciples to get on the step which is next for them, and not to suggest to them to jump through a flight of steps.

27. Do not neglect the Lamb, for without Him one cannot see the Gate.

And no one will be able to come to the King remaining "naked".

The *sacrificial Lamb* is Jesus Who went to His cross death in order that the knowledge, left by Him, save people from hell.

The second phrase of this fragment is a continuation of the idea from fragment 23. The "naked" ones are those who show off on the surface of the Earth in material bodies identifying themselves with the bodies and thinking that what they do in secret from other embodied people will be a secret for all. But in fact, they are in full view of all spirits and God. In fact, they are laughable as if they stay naked among other embodied people and do not notice their nudity.

But one cannot visit the King in a body, thinking about oneself as of the body. One can go to the King only not identifying oneself with the body, only having achieved the real freedom from it through meditative training. Indeed, the stages of meditative practices (meditation is work on the development of the consciousness) allow one to receive the true baptism and not the "toylike" one, allow one to be born and become mature in new eons.

28. The Man of Heaven has many more Sons than an earthly man. If the sons of Adam are many, al-

though they die, how much more are the Sons of the Perfect Man, Those Who do not die and are begotten again and again!

The Perfect Man is Christ. His Teachings — at the cost of His cross death and the work of His apostles — remained on the Earth and continue to beget new and new spiritual Children, Who achieve immortality in the Abode of the Father.

29. The Father created a Son, but a Son cannot create a son. Because the One Who was born in that way (by the Father) cannot beget. A Son makes brothers for Himself, not sons.

The earthly reproduction is not attractive to a Son of God. Therefore, He begets not earthly children, but spiritual ones — brothers and sisters.

30. This part of the original text is damaged.

31. There are those who feed from a mouth if the word of God comes from it. If one feeds like this — one can become Perfect.

The Perfect can be conceived by a kiss and be born thus.

For this reason, we also kiss one another to become conceived from the grace which is in each one of us.

A Perfect Teacher feeds disciples with the word of God from the mouth. And this can bring them to the Perfection.

Having been prepared by previous incarnations, psychogenetically mature disciples can be awaked to further advancement by Love of the Teacher. And then they can be born in the highest eons.

The emotions of tender love help disciples in their spiritual work, supporting, inspiring, and imbuing them with power.

32. There were three who always walked with the Lord: Mary — His mother, His sister, and Mary Magdalene — who was called His companion. So, there were three Marys: His mother, His sister, and His companion.

33. *The Father* and *the Son* are single names.

But *the Holy Spirit* is a Double name. For They are everywhere: They are above, They are below, They are in the hidden space, They are in the open (space).

(At that) the Holy Spirit is open below and hidden above.

The Holy Spirit, coming from the Abode of the Father, is present in His different states above the surface of the Earth ("the open space") and inside our planet ("the hidden space").

However, the Holy Spirit below the surface of the Earth can be seen by a spiritual warrior and can be invisible above it to a worldy person.

34. Saints are served by evil powers as well. These powers are blind because of the Holy Spirit: they think that they serve their men, but in fact they work for the saints.

Once, a disciple asked the Lord about something of this world. The Lord answered him: "Ask your mother — she will give you of the things which are alien to Me".

The coarser in their energy nature individual conscious-nesses are, the coarser and farther from God-the-Father are the eons where they live during their non-incarnate state. They have no ability to enter the abodes of more perfect con-sciousness and do not see those who live in the eons more close to the Father.

But more perfect creatures of the spiritual world are able not only to enter coarser eons, but also to control their in-habitants, at that, the latter may not even know about this.

God personally or through worthy spirits controls all other spirits and embodied people, including the most prim-itive ones. And they are used by Him for correcting other embodied people — both sinful and righteous, for example, when the latter need to reform, to be redirected, and so on.

35. The apostles said to their disciples: "Let all our gifts contain salt". By salt they called wisdom. Without it, one's giving must not be performed.

The apostles advised disciples to not merely give, for example by healing, but to accompany this with preaching the Path to the Perfection. Without this, a spiritual person should not give, because such gifts will not bring real ben-efits to their receivers.

36. But wisdom cannot be well-grounded with-out a Son...

Then the original text is damaged.

The true Wisdom can originate only from God-the-Fa-ther. And the most perfect Mediator of the Father's Wisdom is His Son-Christ.

37. What the Father possesses belongs also to His Son. While the Son is small, He is not entrusted

with what belongs to Him. But when He becomes adult, the Father gives Him all that is His.

Incarnated in a body, an infant Christ cannot manifest all His Divine abilities. They are given to Him as His earthly body matures.

38. Those people who go astray from the Path were born on the Earth also according to the will of the Spirit of God. Yet, they go astray from the Path also according to His will. Thus, lamps are kindled and put out by the same Spirit.

First, God puts obstacles on the Way to Him: by overcoming them we develop ourselves. And only those people who are worthy, i.e. mature enough, can overcome these obstacles.

Second, there is another point that God possesses all the Power and Authority necessary for preventing unworthy people from approaching His eons: no one can enter the Abode of the Father against His Will.

The worthiness of spiritual warriors is determined from the ethical and intellectual criteria, which are closely related with each other, and from the degree of the subtlety of the consciousness.

39. There is simple wisdom. But there is also wisdom consecrated by death: this wisdom has cognized death. The wisdom which has not cognized death is small wisdom.

Most people live on the Earth not thinking about the fact that our opportunity to change our own destinies for hundreds (usually) years between incarnations and for the next incarnation (if it will take place) is limited in time. Later, it will be impossible even to dream about such a change.

But if people live remembering about the coming end of the incarnation, then this prompts them to advance on the spiritual Path and allows them to differentiate perfectly between that which has value and that which has not — in front of the coming death.

The most radical and effective decision of a spiritual warrior, for whom the knowledge about death has become an ally, is the decision to master the control over death through developing the ability of dematerializing the body.

If such a person has went also through clinical death and has been to the *other world* without impediments from the physical shell, then this becomes a very essential addition to the meditative experience, it provides absolutely reliable knowledge about life there and about what is necessary to do in order to fulfill everything to the maximum.

40. There are animals devoted to man like cows, donkeys, and others. And there are those not devoted to man, which live apart in the desert.

Man plows in the field with the help of devoted animals. Thanks to this, man provides with food both oneself and the devoted animals, but not those undevoted.

In the same way, the Perfect Man works with the help of those who are faithful and prepares everything that is necessary for their being. Thanks to this, everything is at the right place: the good and the bad, the right and the left.

But the Holy Spirit takes care of everyone and controls everything: the faithful, the hostile, and the indifferent. He unites them and separates them in order that they all may gain power when He decides it is necessary.

The Holy Spirit, who acts from the Abode of the Father, is the Main Supervisor of the destinies of embodied people. For realization of their destinies He, in particular, directs thoughts, desires, corrects even the fulfillment of different physical deeds of people, arranging in that way meetings of people with each other. Thus He brings together disciples with teachers, criminals — with their victims, those seeking a sexual partner — with their future partners, and so on. But He also separates people using the same methods when their relations become unnecessary from the standpoint of their spiritual advancement.

He controls the faithful and the unfaithful to Him, the good and the evil ones, those who know Him and those who do not know.

But for us, of course, it will be easier and more pleasant, as well as more efficient, to learn from Him if we become disciples who love Him and the Father.

An incarnate Perfect Teacher, of course, is more convenient for the disciples, because He or She speaks with them in an easy-to-understand language. But, on the other hand, such an earthy Mission is more difficult for the Teacher, because embodied in earthy hell He or She is attacked by many evil people. Therefore, such a voluntary incarnation is a manifestation of the Teacher's Great Sacrificial Love.

Due to understandable reasons, such Teachers teach directly only those who are faithful to Them.

41. This part of the original text is damaged.

42. First, adultery takes place, then a murderer is born from it. He was a son of a devil before, therefore, he becomes a murderer of people now and kills his brothers.

Every (sexual) intercourse of dissimilar people is adultery.

Adultery is a sexual intercourse of people which is improper from God's standpoint. This notion has nothing to do with the one used by "pastors" of many Churches to intimidate their "flock", they try to control people's destinies on behalf of God, though God did not entrust this to them!

From God's standpoint, there is a concept of adultery. And He can even punish for committing it, as we have read in this fragment, by incarnating a devilish soul to the body of a child to be born, or through birth of ugly children, imbeciles, and so on.

God is not against sex in general. It is according to God's design that the population of human bodies on the Earth is maintained thanks to sex. Through sexual interactions people also learn — under the guidance of the Holy Spirit — what kind of a person they should be and what kind they should not be. Sexual relations between people are also a means by which God teaches us love, wisdom, and power.

The most general principles of correct behavior in the sphere of sexual relations are:

— tactfulness, abandonment of egoism, acting not for oneself, but for the sake of the partner, for the sake of mutual harmony,

— abandonment of coarseness in emotions, words, deeds; attempts to cultivate in oneself and to give to the beloved subtle tenderness — the most precious emotion on the Path to Perfection.

May one change partners? Or must one live the whole incarnation with one partner? The answer is: of course, one may! Because by changing partners we can learn much more in the art of giving our love.

However, birth of children certainly imposes duties on both parents.

But if one is obsessed with seeking sexual pleasure, having forgotten about everything else, this will be the sin of adultery, and God will point out this mistake, for example, by inflicting venereal diseases.

In the second paragraph of this fragment, the Author writes about another kind of adultery, and this is related, first of all, to people who already walk the spiritual Path.

It concerns the adequacy of the partner. An adequate partner is not just the one whom you like and who agrees with you, and with whom everything goes well (though this is also important). But the partner must be a like-minded person and a companion on the Path to the Father.

If there is a significant difference in the age of souls, in the degree of the energetical refinement of the organisms and subtlety of the consciousnesses, if one of the partners is not firm in following the *killing-free* nutrition, which is the only ethically and bioenergetically correct one, then such relations will be a serious obstacle for the other partner who is more faithful and closer to God. And this will be adultery from God's standpoint, i.e. an inadmissible and punishable act.

43. God is like a dyer. Just as good dyes, which are called colorfast, get destroyed only with the things dyed in them, it is the same with God. Because His dyes do not fade, they are immortal thanks to His work of the "dyer".

God baptizes those whom He baptizes in the Flow.

The first baptism, given by God, happens in the Flow of the Holy Spirit. God gives it only to the worthy. At that, the baptism transforms them so that the "dyes" are never washed out.

44. It is not possible to perceive anything of the Imperishable unless one becomes like It.

In the world of the True Life, everything happens not in the same way as among earthly people: they perceive the sun, although they are not the sun, they perceive the sky and the earth and all other objects, not being them.

But in *that* world, you perceive something, and you become it. Thus you perceive the Holy Spirit, and you become Him. You perceive a Christ, and you become a Christ. You perceive the Father, you become the Father.

In that world you perceive everything, but you do not perceive yourself. But you perceive yourself as That One, because you become the One Whom you see.

Philip shares His personal impressions from the highest meditations, which Jesus taught, from the meditations of Mergence, in particular.

45. Faith begs. Love gives.

One must not receive without faith. One must not give without love.

Therefore, in order to beg we believe, and in order to give truly we love.

But the one who gives without love does not benefit from such giving.

46. The one who has not received the Lord yet is still a Hebrew.

These words were written for readers-Hebrews. Their meaning is:

The one who cognized God stops experiencing oneself as a representative of particular nationality, religious, sexual, or age group: all these become things of the past, there is only experience of oneself as a consciousness, aspiring to the Beloved.

47. The first apostles called Him thus: Jesus Nazarene Messiah, that is Jesus Nazarene Christ. The last word is Christ, the first is Jesus, in the middle — Nazarene.

The word Messiah has two meanings: Christ and King. Jesus in Hebrew means Savior. Nazara is Truth. Nazarene is the One Who came from the Truth.

So, Christ is King. Thus, Nazarene is King and Jesus is also King.

48. A pearl, even if it is cast down into the mud, is not despised. And if one covers it with balsam, it does not become more valuable. But this perl is always valuable to its owner.

It is the same with the Sons of God: wherever They may be, They are still of value to Their Father.

49. If you say, "I am a Jew!" — no one will move. If you say, "I am a Roman!" — no one will be disturbed. If you say, "I am a Greek, a barbarian, a slave, a free man!" — no one will flinch. But if you say, "I am a Christian!" — everyone will tremble. Oh, if I could receive this rank, which is unbearable for the earthly rulers!

50. God is an Eater of men. Men are consumed by Him.

Formerly men sacrificed animals. But their souls were consumed not by God.

The meaning of that which we call organic life on the planet Earth consists in the development of consciousness embodied in its containers — in living bodies.

Having began their evolution as primitive energetic microformations on the lattice of minerals, having passed then through many incarnations in vegetal, animal, and human bodies, some souls become finally Godlike and infuse themselves into the Creator — the Primordial Universal Consciousness, thus being consumed by Him. This constitutes His Evolution. We are its participants.

Moreover, spiritually developed people, at the final stages of the personal evolution, sacrifice themselves, their individualities — for the sake of Merging in Love with the Consciousness of the Universal Father. For such people it is natural: because they are in the state of highest love for the Highest Beloved! From the outside, it may seem as sacrificial self-annihilation.

In ancient times, the echoes of wishes of God about sacrificial love reached the human masses. And people began to kill animals as a sacrifice to Him, eating afterwards their corpses and offering souls as a gift to God or to imaginary "gods".

Jesus Christ was against such primitivism, suggesting that people must refuse killing animals as a "sacrifice to God" or for using their bodies for food.

51. Glass vessels and clay vessels are both made by means of fire. But glass vessels, if broken, can be remade, for they came into being through a breath. Clay vessels, if broken, are thrown away, for they were made without breath.

It is possible to melt down pieces of glass and make from them new vessels. But pieces of burned clay can be only thrown away.

There is a wise allegory here.

Both glass and clay, when used for production, go as if through "baptism in fire".

Glass goes also through "baptism by the breath" (the analogy with the Flow of Pranava), but clay does not. The baptism in Pranava must precede the baptism in Divine Fire. Therefore, "baptism in fire" of clay vessels cannot give a lasting result.

The point here is that in spiritual work it is necessary to move from stage to stage: one must not jump over several stages, it is impossible to remain in the Divine Fire without strengthening oneself first in other variations of Mergence with God.

52. A donkey, walking around a millstone, has walked a hundred miles.

When it was untethered, it remained at the same place.

There are men who walk much, but advance nowhere. And when evening comes for them, they have seen neither city nor village to which they were going, they have cognized neither the nature of the Creation nor the Power (i.e. God-the-Father), nor even angels. Futile was the work of these miserable.

The efforts can yield good fruits only if the Goal and the methods of its cognition are clear. Or it is necessary to take the hand of the Teacher and hold tight to it. (The Teacher is the One Who is capable of leading to the Goal and Who knows It well).

53. Our thanksgiving — to Jesus! In Syriac, He is called Pharisatha, i.e. the One Who exists everywhere.

Jesus came to show the crucifixion of that which belongs to this world.

We have said already about the possibility and necessity not only of qualitative but also of quantitative growth of individual consciousnesses. The consciousness of an ordinary man in the relaxed state is not larger in size than the man's body. But thanks to special meditative training, it can be grown up to sizes comparable to the size of the planet and even larger. Only having fulfilled this (together with many other things), one becomes worthy of entering the eon of the Father.

Jesus traversed this Path long before His incarnation, which is well known to modern people. And He indeed became the One Who exists everywhere. In particular, He, being on the Earth, was at the same time in the Abode of the Father.

He also proved with His cross death and following appearances to His embodied disciples that the consciousness does not die together with the body, that one can sacrifice the body for the sake of realization of the highest goals.

54. The Lord once came to the dye-works of Levi. He took 72 different dyes and threw them into the vat. Then He took all fabrics from it, and they were white. He said, "Even so the Son of Man works".

Philip describes one of the miracles performed by Jesus. By this miracle Jesus showed to the disciples the following principle of the work of a Teacher: at the beginning very different (multicolored) disciples should be "whitened" in the common "vat" of the spiritual School, they should become white as souls — as the Fire of the Father.

The phrase "the Son of Man", by which Jesus often called Himself, means: "A part of the Father embodied among people in a body born by a woman".

55. A woman who has not given birth to children may become a mother of angels. Such a woman was Mary Magdalene, a companion of the Son. The Lord loved her more than He loved all other disciples and often kissed her on her mouth. The other disciples, seeing Him loving Mary, said, "Why do You love her more than us?". Answering them, He said, "Why do I not love you as her?".

This fragment describes, in particular, the relationship between Jesus and His favorite female disciple (i.e. the best of His female disciples) Mary Magdalene. This relationship was filled with tender and affectionate emotionality. Demonstrating this to His disciples, Jesus gave an example of optimal relationships between people in common spiritual work. United by the emotions of love-tenderness, a group of worthy disciples works much more effectively. Relationships between the Teacher and disciples can be of the same kind.

56. When a blind person and a sighted person are both in the darkness, they are not different from each other.

But when light comes, then the one who sees will see the light, and the one who is blind will remain in the darkness.

When a Teacher from God comes, only those capable of seeing the Divine Light awake for the spiritual life; the rest remains in their darkness of ignorance.

57. The Lord said, "Blessed are those who verily existed before were born (on the Earth).

"The one who verily exists now was like this and will be."

Jesus said about the evolution of units of consciousness.

Psychogenetically young people can live only an instinctive-reflexive life similar to the life of primitive animals.

Those who represent a qualitatively and quantitatively developed Consciousness are capable of truly conscious, rightly directed, disciplined existence on the Path to spiritual Perfection, on the Path to the Father.

But the maturing of the consciousness is a quite slow process, and it lasts many incarnations.

The more mature people are the fewer mistakes they make, and they have fewer chances to fall down from the stairway of spiritual ascent. The statement of Jesus is about this: first, for such people who come into this earthly life being mature enough it is easy to live. Second, if we see such people, this means that they were prepared to such a level of existence before the beginning of the present incarnation.

58. The superiority of man is secret: man has mastery over animals, which are stronger than man is, which are greater by appearance and power. However, it is man who provides them with food. But if man moves away from them, they begin to bite, slay each other. And they will eat each other if they do not find any food.

But now they will have food because man has tilled the soil.

In this parable, mankind on the Earth (mankind which consists mostly of psychogenetically young and immature people) is likened to domestic animals in the "Estate" of God. Despite the fact that animals obey the Master, nevertheless they remain beasts in relations with each other if they are given freedom of actions, and particularly, if there is a lack of food for them.

The Author of this parable hoped that now when Man-God Christ gave people the true and eternal spiritual food

— all people-beasts will be satisfied and will stop being beasts...

59. If those who were immersed in the Flow and having received nothing in It say nevertheless "I am a Christian!", then they take this name on credit.

But if one has really received the baptism in the Holy Spirit, then such a person has the name 'Christian' as a gift.

The one who received a gift does not have to give it back, but from the one who received a credit, this credit may be taken back.

John the Baptist performed the rite of the water baptism for repentant sinners.

Jesus and the apostles baptized with the Holy Spirit, asking Him to manifest Himself by influencing the consciousnesses of the baptized people. (Let us notice that it is not equal to the birth in the Holy Spirit).

The esoteric meaning of such a baptism is to give beginners the first experience of what the Holy Spirit is. In the future, the memory about this experience can inspire the baptized to dedicate the life to changing oneself according to this Standard, to strive for attainment of Mergence with the Holy Spirit.

But other people, who just stood during the baptism and got nothing, nevertheless, assume the title of Christians for themselves. If they in addition will not work on self-improvement in order to become worthy of being Christians, then they will be considered debtors who did not repay their debts to God, burdening thus their destinies.

60. The mystery of marriage is similar to this.

Those who are in a pure marriage are honorable. For without this, one cannot find peace.

Man is the main essence of everything on the Earth. And the main (earthly) function of man is marriage.

Cognize the pure marriage, for it has great power!

As for its impure form, it exists only as an outer appearance.

We have said already that a marriage is a remarkable opportunity for self-development of people longing for the Truth.

We have also discussed what adultery is. It happens: a) when people are obsessed with seeking pleasure — to the detriment of their duties before God and other people, and b) when partners, engaged in sexual relations, are too different from each other from the standpoint of their spiritual advancement, i.e. partners that need to study in the School of God in different programs, not in the same one.

And now we have to consider what marriage is.

There is a state registration of matrimonial relations. It fixes de jure spouses' relations concerning their property and the rights of children. Such social regulation of marriage is absolutely correct for most people who follow only self-interest and discharge their obligations to other people only under the compulsion of law.

There are also Church marriages. Some Churches assume the right to give or not to give permission for sexual relations between people, allegedly on behalf of God. Why? — Because Church leaders want to keep the "flock" in awe and obedience.

But God calls by husband and wife those two who form a firm spiritual union, the sexual relations are a component of this union. God wishes to manage these affairs of people Himself: whom to unite and when, and whom to split. He does this very easily, for example, by regulating the emotions of the partners towards each other.

Defiled forms of matrimonial relations can exist not only in the two forms of adultery mentioned above but also in the disgusting qualities of one or both spouses: such as egoism, harshness, arrogance, violence towards the partner in sexual and other relations, and the desire to offend and insult the partner.

61. Among evil spirits there are both male and female ones. Male ones long for uniting with the souls which inhabit female bodies, and the female spirits — with souls in male bodies, with those who live alone.

And no one can run away from such spirits when they seize an embodied soul, unless they combine in themselves the power of man and woman, i.e. in a marriage. Thus, one receives this power in a marriage, which is a symbolic prototype of uniting in the Bridal Chamber.

When primitive women see a man, sitting alone, they come to him, flirt with him, and defile him. In the same way primitive men, when they see a beautiful woman sitting alone, molest, rape, and defile her.

But if they see a husband and a wife sitting nearby, they do not approach them.

In the same way, it can be when one unites with the consciousness with an angel — then no evil spirit dares to come to such a man or woman.

Those who have come out of the earthly cannot be seized by evil spirits, as it can happen when one is in the earthly. Now they are above passion… and fear. They become masters of their own nature; they are above earthly desires.

... Sometimes it happens that evil spirits see a single man and seize him, torture him... And how can he escape them, being subjugated by his own desires and fear? Where can he hide from them?...

It happens often that some people come and say, "We want to become believers in order to get rid of evil spirits and demons"... But if the Holy Spirit had been with them, then no evil spirit would have cleaved to them!

In this fragment, Philip, in a parable-allegory manner peculiar also to Jesus, brings the reader to the idea of "Marriage", Mergence, similar to conjugal one, of one's consciousness with the Consciousness of the Father in the Bridal Chamber. This provides, in particular, full protection from evil spirits.

On the early stages of the Path to God-the-Father, spiritual warrior can receive the protection through real connectedness of the consciousness with the Holy Spirit or just with a pure spirit-angel.

62. Do not fear the flesh, nor love it.
If you fear it, it will become your master.
If you love it, it will devour and subjugate you.

One can solve this problem radically only by switching the attention to the Highest Goal — God-the-Father.

63. Either to live in the material world — or to rise in the highest eons! But not to be found *outside!*

In this world, there is good and bad. However, that which is considered good in fact is not good. And that which is considered bad in fact is not bad.

Verily the bad exists outside of this world of matter! It is that which is outside. It is perdition there.

While we live in this world, it is necessary for us to acquire the Resurrection, so that when we strip off the flesh, we may be found in Calm, not walk outside.

Yet many go astray from the Path.

It is good to leave this world having not committed sins!

64. There are people who neither desire nor can work (on self-improvement).

Others desire but do not do this. And therefore, they do not benefit from such a desire. This only makes them sinners.

As for those who can but do not desire, they will get their deserts: both for the lack of desire and for the lack of deeds.

65. This part of the original text is damaged.

66. The beginning of this fragment in the original text is damaged.

... I am speaking not about the fire which has no manifestation (i.e. symbolic, mythic), but about the real one, which is white, which radiates the beautiful Light, which gives the Truth.

It is about a manifestation of God in the form of Divine Fire. It is quite real. But one can see It only with the eyes of the developed Consciousness, and not with the eyes of the body.

67. The Truth is not given to this world in clear form, but in symbols and images. It is not possible to give It in other forms.

So, there are a birth (in the highest eons) and its symbolic image (an earthly birth). One has to reconstruct the Truth through this image.

Or: what is the Resurrection in reality?

In that way, image after image, man rises.

The same is with the Bridal Chamber: image after image, comes the Truth, which is Mergence.

I say this to those who are not just interested in the words "the Father, the Son and the Holy Spirit", but who gain Them truly for themselves.

But those who do not gain Them thus — then even these words will be taken from them.

Verily, one can gain Them by the blessing of God in the realization of all the fullness of the power of the Cross, which was called by the apostles the *Right-and-Left*.

The One, Who has cognized this, is no longer a Christian but a Christ.

Sometimes it is difficult to find appropriate words peculiar to the material world, when speaking about the phenomena of the highest eons. Therefore, there is no other way but to use symbols and images. They become quite clear to those spiritual warriors who have matured to realize them in meditation.

In the last paragraph, Philip describes — again in symbols and images — one of the highest meditations, which is performed in the highest eons. The One Who masters it in the eon of the Father becomes soon a Christ.

68. The Lord has everything important in the form hidden from this world: the baptism, the blessing,

the transfiguration, the purification, and the Bridal Chamber.

As we already saw from the written above, the outer ritual forms and outer descriptions have nothing in common with the true realization of the things mentioned in this fragment.

69. The Lord said, "I came to bring the lowest to the Highest and the outer — to the inner. And to unite them THERE."

He said about THAT place in symbols and images.

Those who say that God is above are wrong. Because about Him, Who is in That place, one may say that He extends below. And at the same time, He to Who belongs also everything hidden from this world — He is above everything!

In fact, it is just nattering: "the inner and the outer, the outer from the inner"...

Also the Lord called the place of destruction the *outer darkness*. And the entire world is surrounded by it...

He also said, "My Father Who is in the hidden".

He also said, "Go into your chamber, close the door, and address your Father Who is in the hidden". That is — to the One Who is in the *depth* beneath everything.

But the One Who is in the *depth* beneath everything is the Primordial Consciousness. Beyond Him, there is no one residing deeper.

Also they say about Him: "He Who is above everything".

God-the-Father is the Primordial Consciousness, existing throughout the whole universe. He is above and below, and in all sides, and beneath each object of the material world, including our bodies.

He is in the *depth* beneath everything, in the deepest, primordial eon.

So, He can be cognized not above, to which direction people usually raise their hands and eyes, but in the *depth* of the developed spiritual heart, grown up to galactic size.

Having cognized the entrance to His eon, one becomes able to come through it to any point of space, including the points beneath one's own body.

In the last two paragraphs of this fragment, there is a typical of this Gospel "play on words". Its meaning is the following: He Who is beneath everything rules everything.

70. Before Christ's coming, many people came out (from this world). They could not return (immediately) to the place from which they came out. And they could not come out (immediately) from the place to which they came.

But Christ came. And now those who came in can come out, and those who came out can return.

Christ helped His disciples to become closer to Perfection. And now they can, during meditations, leave the world of matter, visit the highest eons, and return again to the world of matter.

Moreover, some of them, being stoned to death for their sermons, afterwards came to their bodies and continued working in them.

Jesus and the apostles also raised the "dead" to their earthly bodies.

71. When Eve was in Adam, there was no death. When she was separated from him, death appeared. If she enters in him again and he accepts her, there will be no death anymore again.

This is again a witty "play on words" with a great meaning. The point is that Adam and Eve are not the names of the first two humans, as it is said in the contradictory ancient Jewish fairy tale included in the Bible. *Adam* means just man, in the aggregate sense of this word. *Eve* means life.

When life, i.e. soul, leaves the body, clinical death happens. But the soul can return to the body.

72. "My God, My God, why, O Lord, have You forsaken Me?" He said these words on the cross.

Then He separated from that place That Which was Divine.

The Lord rose again (in a body) from the dead. He came as He was before. But now His body was perfect, though it was flesh. But this flesh was from the Primordial.

Our flesh is not from the Primordial; we possess only a likeness of it.

Jesus materialized for Himself a new body, which was a concentrated product of pure Divine Energy, in contrast to His former body born by Mary.

73. The Bridal Chamber is not for animals, nor for men-slaves (of passions), nor for women driven by passion.

It is for pure women and men who gained Freedom.

One's birth in the eon of the Father, maturing in it, and Mergence with God-the-Father constitutes the completion of the individual evolution of the soul. Only they can attain this who are highly developed intellectually, ethically, and psychoenergetically, in particular, those who have liberated themselves from earthly passions and attachments, and achieved purity and Divine subtlety of the consciousness.

74. Thanks to the Holy Spirit we are begotten on the Earth.
But we were born again thanks to Christ.
We are baptized in the Holy Spirit.
And after our birth in Him, we united with Him.

The Holy Spirit, Who controls destinies of people, controls also their birth in earthly bodies.

Then the Author speaks about the stages of cognition of the Divine.

The first stage is baptism, when during the appropriate meditation a spiritual warrior enters (or is led in) the appropriate eon and for the first time feels the Consciousness Which dwells there.

Then one has to learn to enter this eon by one's own efforts and stay in it. It is called the birth in it.

And after the birth and the following maturing in this eon — again thanks to mastering special meditative techniques — one comes to Mergence with the Consciousness dwelling in it.

75. Nobody can see oneself, either in a flow or in a mirror, — without light.
And vice versa: you cannot see yourself in the Light without the Flow and without a mirror.
For this reason, it is necessary to be baptized in both: in the Light and in the Flow.

In the Light we receive the blessing.

In this fragment, two points need to be commented.

The first point is the allegorical meaning of the word *mirror*. This is self-examination (looking at oneself) for the sake of discovering vices (with the purpose of getting rid of them) and defects in the development of good qualities (with the purpose of further development of them).

The second point is the word *blessing*. It has two meanings: a) blessing for doing something (analogue — "to give okay") and b) transmission of good energy to another person. The full blessing of a Teacher is when both components are merged together.

Practically, in the Light we can receive the highest bliss and the blessing with the instructions on providing spiritual help to embodied people and blessing with particular pieces of advice about entering the eon of the Father.

76. There were three buildings in Jerusalem for making sacrifice. The one, opened to the west, was called *the holy*. Another, opened to the south, was called *the holy of the holy*. The third, opened to the east, was called *the Holy of the Holiest*, the place where a priest enters alone.

The baptism is *the holy*.

The redemption of others (through one's own sacrificial service) is the *holy of the holy*.

But *the Holy of the Holiest* is the Bridal Chamber.

In the middle of this fragment the original text is damaged.

… What is a bridal chamber if not a symbolic image of the Bridal Chamber? The latter is above all evil.

Its veil is rent from the top to the bottom, as an invitation for the chosen to enter.

In the last paragraph, Philip speaks about the symbolic meaning of the fact that the veil (curtain) in the Jerusalem temple was rent from the top to the bottom at the moment of the cross death of Jesus.

The most important stage preceding one's entering the Bridal Chamber is sacrificial service to God through spiritual service to people.

77. Evil spirits do not see and cannot seize Those Who dressed Themselves with the Perfect Light.

Let such dressing with the Light be secret Mergence.

According to these recommendations, the first task of spiritual warriors is to arise in the eon of Light.

The second is to become mature in it, to become a sufficiently large, active, and able consciousness.

The third is to merge with the Consciousness of this eon.

Evil spirits do not see Those Who dressed Themselves with the Light, but only when They stay in the eon of Light.

78. If the woman had not separated from the man, she would not have died along with the man. The separation from him was the beginning of death.

Therefore, Christ came to correct the separation, to unite them, and to give the True Life to those who died in separation, uniting them.

Philip again jokingly refers to the biblical fairy tale about Adam and Eve. The explanation will be given in the next fragment.

79. So, let a woman unite with her husband in the Bridal Chamber. Because Those Who have united in the Bridal Chamber will no longer be separated.

Eve separated from Adam because she united with him not in the Bridal Chamber.

The true and eternal mergence of the Perfect happens in the Bridal Chamber of the Father.

80. This part of the original text is damaged.

81. On the bank of Jordan, Jesus revealed (to John the Baptist) the Primordial Consciousness of the Kingdom of Heaven, Which was before the beginning of everything. Later He appeared (to John) again. Then He manifested Himself as a Son (of the Heavenly Father). Then He was blessed (by the Father to serve people). Then He was taken by the Father (from this world). Then He began to take (to the Father).

82. Since it is allowed to me to reveal this mystery, I say: the Father of everything united (in the Bridal Chamber) with the Bride Who afterwards came down (to crucified Jesus), and the Light illuminated Him then. And He (leaving that place) came to the Great Bridal Chamber. Therefore, His body, which appeared in the next days, came out from the Bridal Chamber. This body was similar to a body born from a unity of husband and wife (i.e. similar to a usually born body). Jesus made in it (in His new body) everything similar to the image (of a usual body).

It is necessary that each disciple enter the Chamber of the Father.

83. Adam came into being from two virgins: from the (Holy) Spirit and from the uninhabited Earth.

Therefore, Christ was born from (only) one virgin to rectify the mistake which occurred in the beginning.

This is irony, nothing more.

84. There are two trees in the midst of paradise. From one of them originate animals, from another — men. Adam ate of the tree which originates animals. He became an animal and then brought forth animals.

Therefore at present, animals like Adam are held in respect.

So, the tree of which Adam ate a fruit is the tree of animals. This is why his children became so numerous. And all of them also ate the fruits of the tree of animals.

As a result, the fruits of the tree of animals begot numerous people-animals who now honor only man-animal.

But God creates Men. (And these) Men create God.

The greater part of this fragment is irony, this time — bitter. Such a mood of Phillip is especially understandable because of the recent killing of Man-Christ by people-animals.

But the last paragraph in the end of the parable deserves to be analyzed seriously.

From God-the-Father Men-Christs come. They hasten the evolution of individual consciousnesses on the Earth, and by this They contribute to the fast arrival of high quality "Food" (see fragments 50 and 93) into the Father.

85. Earthly people also create "gods" and worship their creations. So let these "gods" worship these people — it will be just!

This is irony regarding pagans inventing gods for themselves. So let the invented "gods" look after these people!

86. The deeds of man result from man's power. Therefore, they are regarded as efforts.

But man also begets children, which are conceived in calm.

The power of man is manifested in deeds, and calm — in children.

You may find that man is similar to God in this respect. Because God also performs His deeds (in the Creation) thanks to His Power, but it is in Calm that He begets His Children.

The sexual function can be realized fully only in deep calm of both partners. Therefore, Philip speaks about children as about the result of the calm of people.

The state of the Consciousness of the Father in the Bridal Chamber is the deepest tender Calm. His Sons and Daughters come from It.

87. In this world, the slaves serve the free. But in the other world, the free will serve these slaves.

However, the Sons of the Bridal Chamber will serve the sons of earthly marriages.

The Sons of the Bridal Chamber have one and the same name. Calm is Their common estate. And They are in need of nothing.

In this fragment there are three profound themes connected together by the common literal "pattern".

In the first part, there is a theme about the predetermination of the future destiny according to our present behavior. Thus, haughtiness, arrogance, violent attitude, cruelty — disgusting manifestations of the hypertrophied "I" in some people — will be destroyed in them by God through placing these people in the situation of slaves subjected to the power of similar to them people-animals. If such vicious people do not want to struggle with their vices voluntarily, God will have to destroy these vices in them using other disgusting people.

But the Holy Spirits gladly bring Their love to people, serving them.

All, Who have settled in the eon of the Father and merged with Him, are the Father. They have attained everything possible to attain in the universe. And They exist in the blissful highest Calm.

88-89. This part of the original text is damaged.

90. Those who say that they will die first and then rise are in error. If they do not receive the Resurrection while being incarnate, they will receive nothing after leaving their bodies.

It is the same with baptism: it is significant only if it is received by the incarnate.

For changing oneself, one needs to have a material body, which is a "transformer" of energies. Without a material body, a non-embodied soul exists in the state in which it was at the end of its last incarnation. In particular, it cannot move to another eon by its will, and nobody can do this for it.

91. It is I, Apostle Philip, saying: Joseph the carpenter planted a garden because he needed wood for his handicraft. It was he who made a cross from the trees, which he himself planted. And the Child of his semen was hung to that which he had planted.

The Child of his semen was Jesus, and the planted — the cross.

Joseph took care only of the material and received from God a dire symbolic hint.

92. The true tree of life is in the middle of paradise. It is an olive tree, from which blessings come.

It is from this tree that the Resurrection is.

The idea of the previous fragment continues: it was necessary for Joseph to look after not the material trees (or not only after them) but after the paradisiacal *tree of life*, growing beyond this world. Then he could gain the Resurrection.

93. This world is a corpse-eater. And all that is eaten (by humans) is contemptible as well.

But the Truth is a life-eater. Therefore, no one who is nourished by the Truth can die.

Jesus came from that place, and He brought food from there. And to those who desired, He gave thus the (True) Life, and they did not die.

Almost all people of "this world" consider the pleasure of eating food as the most important thing in life. To change their gustatory habits even slightly is beyond the capabilities of most of those who call themselves Christians, despite the direct recommendations of Jesus — not to kill animals for food. The nutrition based on killing animals does not allow — because of bioenergetical laws, not to mention the ethical ones — entering the Bridal Chamber or even the Light of the Holy Spirit.

There is no doubt that it is necessary for us to eat material food, otherwise we cannot do anything on spiritual self-development. But nutrition with the material food must not stand against the nutrition with the food "from the Truth".

94. The beginning of this fragment is damaged in the original text.

... Paradise is the place where I will be told: "Eat this or do not eat that — as you wish!". It is the place where I will eat anything, because there grows the tree of knowledge. It is this tree that destroyed Adam. However, it made man live actively.

The Law (of the Jewish Bible) was this tree. It may suggest what is good and what is bad. But it does not remove man from what is bad and does not strengthen man in what is good. And it created destruction for those who ate of it. For when it commanded, "Eat this, do not eat that!" — this became the beginning of death.

Philip plays in this parable with the biblical story about paradise.

God-Teacher shows to people both what is good and what is bad. Moreover, having explained to people the principles of advancement towards the Highest Goal, He provides them with *freedom of will* — the freedom of choice of where and how to go.

People have to go by themselves, finding the correct Path, developing themselves through this. God only suggests the Path — secretly or obviously, sometimes jokingly. And the choices are made usually by people.

This provides people with experience, maturity, and wisdom. Having obtained wisdom, one can overcome all difficulties and through such struggle become Perfect. Only for such a person the Father will open the door to His Bridal Chamber.

95. The blessing is superior to the baptism, because it is thanks to the blessing that we were called Christians, not thanks to the baptism.

And Christ was called so thanks to the blessing. Because the Father blessed the Son, the Son blessed the apostles, and the apostles blessed others.

The one who was blessed will gain the Resurrection, and the Light, and the Cross, and the Holy Spirit.

To Him (to Christ) the Father gave this (blessing) in the Bridal Chamber; He received this.

96. The Father was in the Son, and the Son was in the Father. Such are affairs in the Kingdom of Heaven.

The second humorous phrase does not provide any significant information, it only stimulates the reader to solve the mystery of the first phrase.

In the first phrase, there is a description of the interaction of the Consciousnesses of the Father and the Son: Mergence, Coessentiality.

97-98. Fragment 97 is damaged in the original text. Fragment 98 contains an idea which is a continuation of the previous one, therefore, it cannot be interpreted as well.

99. This world came into being (probably) by mistake. Because the one who created it wanted to create it imperishable and immortal. But he (probably) died, not attaining his goal, because the world did not become imperishable, as well as the one who created it.

There is no imperishability of the fruits of material deeds, but there is only (imperishability of deeds) of the Sons and Daughters. And there is nothing that can attain Imperishability except a Son and a Daughter.

The one who cannot even accumulate one's own power — how much more such one is unable to help others!

The first part of the fragment is just a joke, which serves as an artistic beginning of the parable.

Then there is a point that the only valuable fruits of all the activity in the entire Creation are Those Who have gained absolute Imperishability and Eternity — the Sons and Daughters of the Heavenly Father, Those Who have entered His Bridal Chamber.

In the end of the fragment, there is an idea that the one who strives to help others must first help oneself through efforts on self-development: the one who can do nothing — how can such one help others?

100. The cup of prayer contains wine and water, serving as a symbol of blood, over which thanks-

giving is performed. And it becomes filled with the Holy Spirit.

It belongs to the Perfect Man (to Christ).

When we drink it, we will become Perfect Men.

To drink the Cup of Christ does not mean to take communion in a church, even if one does it a hundred times.

To drink the Cup of Christ means to walk His entire Path up to the Bridal Chamber, and go through His Calvary.

101. The Living Flow is like the Body (of the Holy Spirit). It is necessary that we dress ourselves in the Living Body. Therefore, if you go and submerge in the Flow, you must become naked so that you may be dressed in It.

The Body of the Holy Spirit is an image that helps meditative perception of the integrity of the Holy Spirit. He is indeed Living, Perceiving, Loving, Guiding, Speaking.

In order to experience the Body of the Holy Spirit, one has to become "naked", to get rid of all shells and layers which are coarser than the Holy Spirit. Thus we find ourselves in the same eon where He is and receive the baptism, birth, and blessing in this eon.

102. A horse begets a horse, a human being begets a human being, God begets God.

The rest of this fragment is damaged in the original text.

103-104. Let me say about the place where the Children of the Bridal Chamber abide.

In this world there is a union of man and woman. This is mergence of energy and calm.

In the highest eon there is another form of a union, we just use the same words. In that eon other Consciousnesses abide, They are above all words, They are beyond anything coarse, dense. This is in the place where the Power (i.e. the Father) is; in the same place are the Chosen of the Power.

Those, Who are there, are not the one and other: They all are *One* there.

And those who live here cannot even leave their fleshly bodies…

Philip explains the symbolism of the text: in the Bridal Chamber of the Father, They do not have sex as incarnate people do. But They merge in Love and exist there as *One*.

105. Not all who have a body are able to cognize their own Essence. And those who cannot cognize their own Essence cannot use the possibilities given to them for enjoyment.

Only those who cognized their own Essence will enjoy truly.

To cognize the highest enjoyment, one has to make great efforts on self-development. Only the one who succeeds in the cognition of the Father attains this.

The cognition of one's own Essence is the realization of oneself as a Consciousness in the Abode of the Father. He is our Higher Self, which is cognized when we infuse ourselves into Him.

106. The Perfect Man cannot be captured (by evil spirits) and cannot be seen by them. Because they can capture only those whom they see.

There is no way to acquire this boon but by being dressed in the Perfect Light and by becoming the Perfect Light. If one becomes dressed in It, one merges with It.

Such is the Perfect Light.

One should seek salvation from evil spirits not in "protective magic", not in cursing them, not in the methods of "bioenergetical protection" or in the incantation of sorcerers, but in Mergence with God.

107. It is necessary that we become men of Spirit before we leave this world (i.e. before the end of this incarnation).

The one who acquired everything in this world, being its master, will not be able to become a master in another world.

Jesus cognized the whole Path up to the end. But, nevertheless, He came to this world as a simple man (i.e. He did not behave like a "master").

108. The Holy Man is holy entirely, down to the body. If one gives bread to the Holy Man, the Holy Man consecrates it, as well as water or anything else that may be given. All this becomes purified. And how will the Holy Man not purify bodies also?

A truly holy Man becomes a natural healer.

109. When performing baptism, Jesus "poured" life into bodies and "poured" death out from them.

Therefore, we submerge now in the Flow (of Life), but not in (the flow of) death, so that we are not carried away by it to the spirits of this world. When these spirits blow, desolation happens. When the Holy Spirit blows, bliss comes.

110. The one who cognized the Truth is free. The free one does not commit sin: because the one who commits sin becomes a slave of sin (i.e. burdens one's own destiny, first of all).

The true knowledge is like a mother and a father (i.e. like wise teachers, advisers, and guardians of their child).

Those who are not capable of sinning are said to they have attained freedom. The knowledge of the Truth raises them even more. This makes them both free and above this world.

But only love creates. The one who becomes free thanks to knowledge, because of Love remains a slave of those who have not managed to attain the Freedom of knowledge yet. Such one brings the knowledge to them and this develops them because it calls them to the Freedom.

Love takes nothing: how can it take something? Everything belongs to it. It does not say, "This is mine! And this is mine!" But it says: "This is yours!"

111. Spiritual love is like wine and myrrh. Those enjoy it who were blessed (by God).

But others also enjoy it — those who stay with the blessed ones. But if the blessed go away, those who are not blessed fall back to their stench.

The Samaritan gave nothing but wine and oil to the wounded man. And it was nothing else but blessing. Thus he healed the wounds.

And love covers a multitude of sins.

It does not make sense to comment shortly this fragment, because its meaning can be comprehended only by those who have personal experience of love-service to a large number of different people.

112. Those born by a woman resemble the man she loved. If he was her husband, they resemble the husband. If he was her lover, they resemble the lover. It happens that she unites with the husband, as she is obliged to do, but her heart is with her lover with whom she also unites, then her children resemble the lover.

But you, who are with the Son of God, do not get attached also to the earthly! Rather be only with the Lord, so that those begotten by you be not similar to the earthly but similar to the Lord!

113. A human being unites with a human being, a horse — with a horse, a donkey — with a donkey. Representatives of any species unite with those similar to them.

In the same way, the Spirit unites with the Spirit, and Logos — with Logos, and the Light — with the Light.

If you become a human being — a human being will love you. If you become the Spirit — the Spirit will unite with you. If you become Logos — you will unite with Logos. If you become the Light — the Light will unite with you.

If you become one of the earthy rulers — the earthy rulers will associate with you. If you become a horse, or a donkey, or a cow, or a dog, or a sheep, or any other animal whether smaller or bigger, you will not be able to associate either with human, or with the Spirit, or with Logos, or with the Light, or with earthly rulers, or with those who under their rule. They will not lie in bed with you, and will not accept your love.

114. Those who were slaves against their will may get freedom.

But those to whom the freedom was granted by the mercy of the lord, but who, nevertheless, put themselves into slavery again, — they will no longer be able to become free.

Christ showed people the Path to full Liberation in the Abode of God-the-Father. But only a few accepted this offer. Well, this is a grievous choice of others…

115. Farming in this world requires four essences: water, earth, air, and light.

In the same way, the farming of God consists of four essences: faith, aspiration, love, and knowledge.

Our "earth" is faith in which we are deep-rooted, "water" is aspiration which carries us, "air" is love thanks to which we live, and "light" is knowledge which allows us to mature.

116. The beginning of this fragment is damaged in the original text.

… Blessed be those who have not caused grief to any being.

Such was Jesus Christ. He greeted all in this world and did not burden anyone with Himself.

Blessed be those who live like this! For they are perfect men!

For Logos is like this.

117. Ask us about Him! For we cannot reproach Him for anything! How can we reproach this Great One? He gave Calm to everyone!

Let us notice: the Great Ones give Calm. The opposite of them, demonic and devilish people bring enmity, hatred, chaos, violence, devastation, suffering.

118. First of all, one should not distress anybody: either big or small, unbeliever or believer; then one should offer Calm to those who live in peace and good.

There are Those Who can give Calm to those living in good.

Mere kind people cannot do this, because they themselves are still dependent.

And They cannot cause grief, (unnecessary) suffering.

But those, who are still on the way to becoming like Them, distress people sometimes.

The One Who has mastered the secrets of Existence brings joy to good people!

However, there are those who grieve and feel angry because of this.

119. A householder has acquired all sorts of things: children, slaves, cattle, dogs, pigs, wheat, barley, straw, grass, dog's food, and best food, and acorns. As a reasonable man, the householder knows which

food is for whom and thus gives bread and olive oil to the children, castor oil and wheat — to the slaves, barley, straw, and grass — to the cattle, garbage — to the dogs, acorns and bran — to the pigs.

So are disciples of God. If they are wise, they comprehend the discipleship. Fleshly forms do not deceive them, and speaking with someone they look at the state of the soul of that person.

There are many animals with human appearance in this world. Disciples of God identify them and give "acorns" to the "pigs", "barley", "straw", and "grass" — to the "cattle", "garbage" — to the "dogs", "sprouts" — to the "slaves", and the perfect "food" — to the "children".

Using images of animals, Philip writes about psycho-classification of people according to the psychogenetic age and the qualities which everyone of them developed during the personal evolution. Each of these groups needs "food" appropriate only to it.

120. There is the Son of Man (Christ), and there is the Son of the Son of Man. The Lord is the Son of Man. And the Son of the Son of Man is the One Who was created by the Son of Man.

The Son of Man received from God the ability to create. But He can also beget.

See explanation after the next fragment.

121. The one who has the ability to create (earthly things) — creates (them). The one who has the ability to beget (children) — begets. The one who creates (earthly things) cannot beget (at the same time).

But the One Who begets can also create. And the One Who creates — also begets. The progeny of such (Perfect) One is this Creation. This (Perfect) One begets also (another progeny) — not earthly children but Likenesses of Oneself.

The one who creates (earthly things) acts openly, not hiding. The one who begets acts secretly, in private. But this progeny is not like the progeny of the (Perfect) One.

The One, Who creates, creates (also) openly. And the One, Who begets, begets the Sons and the Daughters (also) secretly.

This fragment has much "play on words". This can be seen very clearly if one rewrites it without explanations in brackets.

The verb *to create* in the second paragraph means *to materialize*; this concerns the *creation of the world* by the Father and the ability of Christs to materialize different objects. This world created by the Father can be also regarded as His progeny. Both the Father and the Christ beget new Sons and Daughters, They do this secretly from people of the material world.

122. Nobody can know when a husband and a wife united with each other, except themselves. Because their marriage is hidden from the outsiders.

And if an impure marriage is hidden, then how much more a confidential mystery is the pure marriage! It is not fleshly, but pure, it is determined not by passion, but by sober will. It belongs not to the darkness and night, but to the day and light.

A marriage, if exhibited for others, becomes not clear. A wife is considered unchaste not only if she unites with another man, but even if she leaves her bride-bed and is seen by others.

Let her meet only with her parents, friends of the husband, and the children of her bridal chamber; they may enter her bridal chamber every day. But let others dream of hearing her voice there and of enjoying the fragrance of her incenses! And let them be satisfied, like dogs, with the crumbs that fall from the table.

The Husbands and Wives (of God) belong to the Bridal Chamber. One cannot see Them unless one becomes as They are.

No one except the Father can see and know the Greatness of Those Who attained the Bridal Chamber, unless one attains the same level of development.

123. The beginning of this fragment is damaged in the original text.

... Abraham in order to perceive the One Whom he had to perceive performed circumcision of the foreskin, showing by this (symbolically) that we should rid ourselves of the fleshly — that which is of this world.

Then the original text is damaged partly.

... As long as the intestines of man's body are hidden, the body is alive. But if the intestines are uncovered and fall out, the body dies.

It is the same with a tree: while its roots are hidden, the tree blossoms and grows. If the roots are uncovered, the tree withers.

It is the same with any phenomenon in the world, not only in the material but in the hidden one as well. Thus, as long as the root of evil is hidden it grows and is strong. When it becomes known, it begins to bloom. But if its root is uncovered, it perishes.

Therefore, Logos says, "Already the axe lies at the roots of trees! If it does not cut up completely, that which was cut will grow again. Hence, it is necessary to drive the axe deep enough so that it tears out the roots."

And Jesus destroyed those roots in the place where He worked. And He also did this partially in other places.

As for all of us, let us cut into the roots of evil, which we find within ourselves, and tear out evil with its roots from the soul!

We can tear evil out only if we know it. If we are ignorant of it, it will continue to grow its roots and multiply itself in us. Then it will get complete control over us, we will become its slaves. It will enslave us more and more, forcing us to do that which we do not want to do and forcing us not to do that which we want to do... It is very powerful until we know about it in ourselves!

While it exists, it acts. Ignorance of it is the mother of evil in us. Ignorance brings us to death. And those who have not become free from ignorance have not existed yet as (true) people, are not existing, and will not exist!

Those who are in the true knowledge fill themselves with Perfection as the Truth reveals Itself to them.

For the Truth, even as ignorance, — while it is hidden, it rests in itself, but when it is revealed and recognized, it blooms, being praised.

How much more powerful it is than ignorance and errors! It gives us Freedom!

Logos said, "If you know the Truth, it will make you free".

Ignorance is slavery. Knowledge is Freedom.

Seeking the Truth, we discover its seeds within us.

If we unite with It, It will receive us in the Primordial Consciousness.

Philip discusses the mechanism of repentance and insists on the necessity of paying serious attention to the intellectual work.

Repentance is purification of oneself from vices. Two foundations of all our vices are the following:

1. The ability to cause intentionally suffering to other beings (for example, just by "distressing" them); by doing this we manifest our egoism, the "I", and a lack of developed love in ourselves. With the hypertrophied "I" and without developed love, one cannot really approach the Father.

2. The absence of permanent orientation of the attention to the Father, the absence of aspiration to Him.

In connection with this, let us discuss faith. Faith as simple "yes" as an answer to the question "do you believe?" — is too little. The true faith is indeed the permanent and unshakeable remembering about God-Teacher, Who teaches us all the time; it is especially important to remember about this at the moments of critical situations, which are also His lessons for us. The thing which brings one to such a level of faith is large and long intellectual work done under His guidance.

Only thanks to such efforts of spiritual warriors, God becomes for them a Living Reality, and not just a symbol, an abstraction which you are supposed to worship. Thus faith turns into knowledge about Him.

On the highest level of its development, faith changes — necessarily through the stage of knowledge about Him, knowledge of Him — into passionate Love, which alone can help one to become close to Him and then to enter His Abode and merge with Him.

... Penitential work is not just recalling aloud in front of a "father" all your true and imaginary deeds-sins. Penitential work is studying of oneself as a soul and transforming oneself by introspection and self-education. It is necessary to note that "sins" are not the main things we have to struggle with: they are just manifestations of qualities of the soul which are called vices. Therefore, it is vices that one has to struggle against with the help of the axe about which Jesus and Philip told. And this struggle can be launched in full strength only after one realizes God — as a Living Teacher.

... The result of the entire work on purification and development of oneself is one's birth and maturing in the highest eons. As this happens, all the material, fleshly become less and less significant and then is "cut off" completely (at what Abraham hinted by his circumcision).

Then only He remains.

124. Possessing manifest things of the Creation, we regard them as significant and respected, while that hidden from our eyes — we regard as useless and despicable.

But the reality is opposite: manifest things of this world are useless and despicable; but those found in the world hidden from us are significant and worthy of worship.

The mysteries of the Truth are revealed only through symbols and images.

We, born in material bodies on the Earth, get accustomed to looking from the matter of the body at the world of matter around it.

But those walking the Path pointed by Jesus, after being born and having matured in the highest eons, learn to look and see in these eons, and from them.

Philip writes about His own impressions of such seeing.

125. The Bridal Chamber is hidden. It is the innermost.

At first, the veil concealed how God controls the Creation. But when it is rent (for spiritual warriors who come close to it), and the One Who is inside reveals Himself, then one leaves this house of separation (the body). Moreover, it will be destroyed (dematerialized).

... But the Divine of a spiritual warrior does not enter the Holy of the Holiest at once, because It cannot unite (at once) with the Light, with Which It has not been united yet, and with the Primordial Consciousness, the gate to Which has not been opened yet (for entering). The Primordial Consciousness will be under the wings of the Cross and under Its Arms. This meditation will be the saving ark for the spiritual warrior even if the flood comes.

There are some of the companions of Christ who then will be able to enter inside behind the veil together with the High Priest (Christ).

The veil (of Jerusalem temple) was not rent at the top only. If it were so, then the entrance would have been opened only for those who are of high rank (on the Earth). And it was not rent at the bottom only, because then it would have pointed only to the lower ones (of social hierarchy). But it was rent from the top to the bottom.

The entrance is opened also for us who are low, so that we may enter the Treasury of the Truth.

In it, there is the One Who is by right held in high regard, Who is imperishable.

Yet, we make the Way to that place through disdained symbols and ephemeral images. They are disdained by those who hold the earthly glory. Yet, there is Glory above glory, and there is Power above power.

The Perfection opened for us the Treasury of the Truth. The Holy of Holiest was opened for us, and the Bridal Chamber invited us in!

… As long as all this is hidden from people, evil brings them to the futile. And they have not separated it from that which was sown by the Holy Spirit. Such people are slaves of evil.

But when This approached, the Perfect Light embraces everyone (of those who enter It). And those who are in It receive the blessing. Thus slaves become free, and those who were captured become liberated!

126. Every plant which was planted not by My Heavenly Father will be torn out.

Let they who are separate — unite (in the highest eons) having become Perfect!

All Who enter the Bridal Chamber will kindle the Light of Truth more, for They are not begotten in the darkness as those begotten in earthly marriages! The Fire will burn in the night and flare up stronger, because the mysteries of this Marriage are performed in the Light of Day! That Light of Day will never cease (for Them)!

127. If one becomes a Son of the Bridal Chamber, it means that He has cognized the Light (of the Holy Spirit) before.

The one who has not cognized It in the world of matter will not receive It in That place.

The One Who has cognized the Light (of the Holy Spirit) cannot be seen and captured (by evil spirits). And (evil spirits) cannot torment such Perfect Man even (embodied in a body) in the world of matter. Such Perfect Man has cognized the Truth and dwells now in the Abode of the Primordial Consciousness! And It is opened for such Perfect One — in the Light of the Holy Day!

Bibliography

1. Antonov V.V. — Ecopsychology. "New Atlanteans", Bancroft, 2008.
2. Antonov V.V. — The Original Teachings of Jesus Christ. "New Atlanteans", Bancroft, 2008.
3. Okulov A. and others (eds.) — Apocrypha of Ancient Christians. "Mysl", Moscow, 1989 *(in Russian)*.
4. Trofimova M.K. — Historico-Philosophical Questions of Gnosticism. "Nauka", Moscow, 1979 *(in Russian)*.

Design by
Ekaterina Smirnova.

Made in the USA
Lexington, KY
07 February 2015